LAWYER
COLORING BOOK
I PUT
THE LIT IN
LITIGATE

Published by Karelaalia Varun Publishing

I AM BILLING YOU FOR THIS CONVERSATION

I NEVER DREAMED
I WOULD BE A SUPER COOL
LAWYER
BUT HERE I AM
KILLING IT!

SERVING LOOKS *AND* JUSTICE

LAWYER LIFE

I MAKE IT LOOK EASY

FREE *
LEGAL ADVICE

* Advice is not free, normal billing rates will apply

LAWYER

NUTRITION FACTS

AMOUNT PER SERVING: **1 GREAT LAWYER**

% DAILY VALUE*

HARD WORK	1000%
LAZINESS	0%
TALENT	500%
PASSION	100%
DEDICATION	300%
CAFFEINE	110%

*Percentage daily values are based on your unique diet

Made in the USA
Monee, IL
20 January 2024

52094387R00031